Treasure Hunting

Looking for Lost Riches

Revised Edition

by Caitlin Scott

Reading Consultant:
Timothy Rasinski, Ph.D.
Professor of Reading Education
Kent State University

Content Consultant:
Dana Langolf
Mel Fisher Enterprises

capstone

T0052463

Published by Red Brick® Learning
1710 Roe Crest Drive, North Mankato, Minnesota 56003
www.mycapstone.com

Library of Congress Cataloging-in-Publication Data
Scott, Caitlin, 1965–
    Treasure hunting : looking for lost riches / by Caitlin Scott.
    p. cm.
    Summary: Relates true stories of treasure hunters, discussing the tools
they use, secret codes that have led to treasures, laws and regulations regarding
treasure hunting, and some lost treasures still waiting to be found.
    ISBN: 978-0-7368-2783-6 (hardcover)
    ISBN: 978-1-5157-3687-5 (revised softcover)
    1. Treasure-trove—Juvenile literature. [1. Buried treasure.] I. Title.
G525.S368 2003
622'.19—dc21

                            2003005552

Created by Kent Publishing Services, Inc.
Designed by Signature Design Group, Inc.
This publisher has made every effort to trace ownership of all copyrighted
material and to secure necessary permissions. In the event of any questions
arising as to the use of any material, the publisher, while expressing regret for
any inadvertent error, will be happy to make necessary corrections.

Photo Credits:
Getty Images: Bettmann, 8, 29, Jonathan Blair, 9, 10, Katie DeitsMore, 17,
Richard T. Nowitz, 21, Universal History Archive/UIG, 33; iStockphoto:
Deborah Cheramie, 12, JOE CICAK, 46-47; Newscom: CM Dixon Heritage
Images, 15, 30, MIAMI HERALD/KRT, 4; Capstone Press: 7, 25, 29, 39, 40;
Science Source: Sheila Terry, 38; Shutterstock: Fedor Selivanov, 22 Top, melis,
22 Bottom, Palenque, 39, sumire8, Cover, Ventura, 19, www.BillionPhotos.com,
37; Thinkstock: mountaindweller, 36"

Printed in the United States of America.
PA45

Table of Contents

Mel Fisher found pieces of treasure from the Atocha *during his dive.*

— CHAPTER **1** —

Silver and Gold

A pirate buries a chest filled with gold on an island. A ship sinks, taking thousands of silver coins to the ocean floor. Desert winds and sand bury an old tomb filled with priceless jewels. Many treasure hunts start with such stories. But who finds the treasures? And how?

Tales of Treasure

Mel Fisher dreamed of finding treasure. In the 1960s, he moved from his home in California to Florida. He hoped to find one of the many shipwrecks off the coast there.

In 1968, Fisher read the story of the *Atocha* (a-TOW-cha) in a book called *The Treasure Diver's Guide*. The *Atocha* sank in a hurricane near the Matecumbe (mat-uh-KUHM-bee) **Keys** in 1622. Tons of silver and gold were aboard! But no one had ever found the Spanish ship.

---

key: a low island

The First Discovery

Fisher was thrilled. The *Atocha* had sunk right where his own ship was now **docked**. At least, that's what the story seemed to say.

Fisher set out to look for the treasure. He searched and searched. Days, weeks, and months went by. He found nothing.

Then, Fisher met Dr. Eugene Lyon. Lyon was an **historian**. He could read old Spanish writing. He and Fisher made a deal. Lyon would read the old Spanish shipping **logs** to get a better idea where the *Atocha* sank. Fisher would give Lyon $10,000 and a share of the treasure if he found it.

Lyon went to Spain. There, he discovered something. Long ago, *Matecumbe* meant all of the islands off Florida. There were many, many islands. Fisher might never find the right one.

---

dock: to bring a boat up to a platform built out over the water
historian: a person who is an expert about events of the past
log: the record of a ship's voyage

Florida Keys

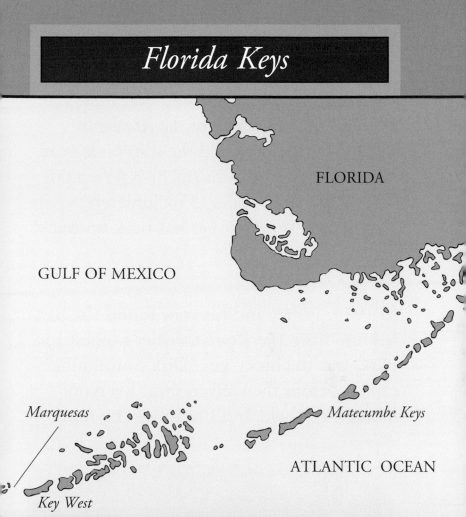

FLORIDA

GULF OF MEXICO

Marquesas

Matecumbe Keys

Key West

ATLANTIC OCEAN

Mel Fisher searched the
Matecumbe Keys for the Atocha.
He finally found the ship near Marquesas.

Back on Track!

Lyon also checked the logs of other ships. He found the log of the ship that first searched for the wreck of the *Atocha* in 1622. These papers said the ship sank near modern-day Marquesas (mahr-KAY-zuhz). This island is 22 miles (35 kilometers) west of Key West. Fisher was back on track!

First Treasure

In 1975, Fisher and his crew found the first treasure from the *Atocha*. Fisher's oldest son, Dirk, was the lucky guy. Dirk found nine cannons from the sunken ship. Everyone thought the gold and silver must be near.

Crewmen raise a bronze cannon from the Atocha *out of the ocean.*

Then Tragedy

Then, something awful happened. Dirk's boat began to leak during the night. The boat sank. Dirk, his wife, and another diver drowned.

Fisher was heartbroken. He wanted to give up the search. But he didn't quit. He knew how badly Dirk had wanted to find the treasure. Dirk would want the hunt to go on.

Some Luck

Coins found on the Santa Margarita

Fisher kept searching. But he still could not find the *Atocha*. In 1980, he did find a different shipwreck, though. It was the *Santa Margarita*, the sister ship of the *Atocha*. This ship's **cargo** wasn't as rich as *Atocha's*. But Fisher did find thousands of gold and silver coins and 43 gold chains. Even this was worth millions.

---

tragedy: a very sad event
cargo: a load of goods carried by a ship

Change in the Law

Meanwhile, the Florida state government learned of Fisher's find. The state wanted the treasure, too. So, it changed the laws. Now, things found in the ocean near the Florida coast belonged to the state.

Fisher was angry. But he didn't give up. He hired a lawyer to fight the new law. It took seven years to win in court. But he got to keep the *Santa Margarita's* treasure. He would also get to keep the *Atocha's* treasure—if he could only find it.

Mel Fisher found these and other treasures on the Santa Margarita.

Treasure at Last

On July 20, 1985, two of Fisher's divers found something. It looked like a **reef**. Then, their **metal detector** went crazy. This was no reef. It was a huge pile of silver bars. Fisher's crew had found the *Atocha*!

There were about 127,000 silver coins, 900 silver bars, 250 pounds of gold, and 700 jewels on board. This huge treasure was worth between $200 and $400 million. It took two years to bring it all up.

It had taken Fisher 16 years to find the *Atocha*. He might have quit many times. But he kept on trying until he found it.

Would you like to be a treasure hunter like Fisher? He had a boat, diving gear, and many helpers. What would you need to hunt for treasure? It depends on where you want to look.

---

reef: a ridge of rock, coral, or sand that lies on the bottom of the water
metal detector: a tool used to show that metal is present

Chapter 2

Treasure Hunting Tools

Many people want to find treasure. But finding it can be hard. Treasure hunters may use special tools to locate treasure. Some tools are costly. Others are cheap. You might even have some treasure hunting tools in your own home!

The Metal Detector

Some treasure is metal or has metal in it. To find it, treasure hunters may use metal detectors. To use a metal detector, the treasure hunter waves this tool back and forth over a certain area. The detector will click or blink when it is near metal. Metal detectors cost from $100 to $500. Some metal detectors will even tell the treasure hunter what kind of metal it has found.

A metal detector is a useful tool that can help searchers find metal underground.

Better than a Hammer

People use metal detectors to find common things, too. In 1992, in Hoxne, England, Peter Whatling was **mending** a fence. Somehow, he lost his hammer. He borrowed a metal detector from his friend, Eric Lawes, to try to find it.

Whatling took the metal detector to the field and waved it over the ground. The metal detector clicked loudly. But it wasn't the hammer that was making the machine click.

Whatling dug into the earth. He found silver coins. Whatling called the British Museum. People from the museum came and dug in the field. They found more gold and silver coins. They also found gold chains, bowls, and vases. The treasure was about 1,500 years old. It had belonged to Romans who once lived in England.

The museum paid Whatling $2.8 million for the treasure. Whatling shared the money with his friend, Lawes.

---

mend: to fix or repair

Peter Whatling found these coins while looking for his hammer.

Simple Digging Tools

Sometimes, treasure is not buried deeply. Treasure hunters can use a simple shovel, hoe, or spade to dig for it. You might have these tools in your home.

Almost anyone who looks for buried treasure uses these simple tools. But diggers must be careful! Such tools are often made of steel. Steel is tougher than silver or gold. Because some treasure breaks easily, treasure hunters must work with care. They don't want to bend, scratch, or break the treasure.

Fields of Gold

In 1948, in Snettisham (SNET-sam), England, a farmer was plowing his field. He turned up a lump of metal.

The farmer could tell the metal was old, so he gave it to a museum. He thought it was worthless. The people at the museum cleaned the metal. It was pure gold!

More people started looking for gold in Snettisham. Using simple digging tools, they found rings, necklaces, coins, and more. The museum paid the people for their finds.

The last treasure in Snettisham was dug up in the 1990s. The museum said all the treasure once belonged to the Celts. The Celts lived in England more than 2,000 years ago.

Teams of Diggers

Sometimes, treasure is buried deep in the earth. But treasure hunters don't know the exact place where. A treasure hunter might use a team of workers to help search. The treasure hunter tells the team where to work. Then, they start digging.

This is the most costly way to look for treasure. Each worker must be paid. No one knows how long it may take to find the treasure. Workers may dig for years and never find a thing.

A worker digs for treasure.

Teamwork Finds a Tomb

Howard Carter may be the most famous hunter of buried treasure. Carter searched for the tomb of King Tut. Tut was a boy king who lived in Egypt about 3,000 years ago. Historians said Tut was buried with all his gold.

Carter hired a team of diggers. His friend, Lord Carnarvon (carn-AH-von), paid them. They searched for King Tut's tomb for many years. But they found nothing. Carnarvon got upset. What if they never found a thing?

Carnarvon told Carter to quit. But on November 4, 1922, the team found what looked like a step. It was the entrance to Tut's tomb! The team dug for two days. Finally, they uncovered the last step. Beyond it was a door. Inside, they discovered Tut's treasure. It was the richest tomb ever found. Carter couldn't have found it alone.

A man wearing scuba gear jumps off a boat.

Scuba Gear

Finding treasure underwater takes special **skill** and **equipment**. Scuba gear lets divers go deep underwater. The divers wear air tanks on their backs. Tubes and facemasks let air flow from the tanks to the divers. The divers can then breathe underwater.

Divers also wear wet suits. These close-fitting suits keep them warm in cold water. The divers wear big flippers on their feet to push the water as they swim.

Jacques Cousteau (koo-STOW) invented scuba gear in 1943. He was a famous diver and scientist. Today, scuba gear costs from $1,000 to $3,000 to buy.

---

skill: an ability that comes from training
equipment: special tools needed for some purpose

Diving for the *Whydah*

Barry Clifford used scuba gear to search for the *Whydah*. This ship sank off the Cape Cod coast of Massachusetts in 1717. It belonged to the pirate Black Sam. Black Sam had stolen lots of silver and gold. His ship was filled with **loot**.

Clifford's ship had a metal detector. It beeped when there was metal near it in the water. This happened often. When it beeped, divers put on scuba gear. Then, they swam down to the ocean floor to see what the metal was. Most of the time, it was just trash like an old anchor or a **tackle box**.

One day in 1984, the detector found something better than trash. It was a cannon. Was it from the *Whydah*? The crew didn't know. They kept diving and bringing up parts of a ship. Finally, they found a bell. It had the name *Whydah* on it. They had found Black Sam's treasure!

---

loot: something stolen or taken by force
tackle box: a container where tools or equipment are stored

These Spanish coins are from the pirate ship Whydah.

Where Can You Find Treasure?

So, now you know some of the tools treasure hunters use. But, how do treasure hunters know where to look?

Sometimes, people tell them about treasure. Other times, it's trickier. The treasure hunter may even have to solve a secret code. Could you solve a code to find treasure? You are about to try!

Ancient writing may give treasure clues.
*What might these Egyptian **hieroglyphs** mean?*

Sometimes, old books and papers hold treasure clues.

---

hieroglyph: a character used in a system of writing made up of pictures and symbols

— Chapter **3** —

Secret Codes

How do people know where to find treasure?
Sometimes, they hear about it. Or, they may read
something. Some people even find treasure by
mistake. But sometimes, they must solve a code to
find treasure. The next two stories have real treasure
codes. See if you can figure them out!

A Pirate Tale

On a dark night in 1763, people saw lights
on Oak Island. This island is off the coast
of Nova Scotia, Canada. No one lived
there. But pirate ships had been seen in
the area.

For many years after, people said that
pirates had gone to the island that night.
Maybe they had buried a treasure on
Oak Island!

Found and Lost

In 1795, Daniel McGinnis and some friends went to look for this possible treasure on Oak Island. They found a tree with a mark on it. Maybe the treasure was buried there! They dug and dug—nothing. At last, they gave up.

In 1803, McGinnis came back to Oak Island. This time, he had more tools. He dug for many days. One day, as darkness fell, his shovel hit wood. Was it a treasure chest? Was it gold? He would have to wait until morning to find out.

In the morning, McGinnis looked in the hole. Ocean water had filled it in! He must have hit an underground **tidal river**. He dug a second hole nearby. It filled with water, too. Finally, he quit digging. But he kept telling the story of the pirates and their treasure.

---

tidal river: a river whose water level changes with the tide

Mysterious Marks

For many years, people looked for the pirate treasure on Oak Island. One day someone found a stone on the island with **mysterious** marks on it. This is what the marks looked like.

Some people thought this was a code that told where the treasure was. What do you think the code says? Take a minute and try to figure it out. Then turn the page.

---

mysterious: hard to explain or understand

The Money Pit

Here is what some people thought the code said:

> **Forty feet below two million pounds are buried.**

But were people reading the stone the right way? Today, many people have dug on Oak Island. The island is now famous. People call it "the money pit." Many people have spent a fortune trying to find the treasure. But no one has ever found it.

Which Lighthouse?

About 60 years ago, a fisherman told Edward Rowe Snow a treasure story he never forgot.

The fisherman told Snow there was a treasure clue in a book in a lighthouse. But which lighthouse? The fisherman didn't know. He only knew the lighthouse was somewhere off the Cape Cod coast.

Searching the Cape

Snow didn't have time to look right away. But he didn't forget the story. Years later, he came back to search for the treasure.

Snow found an old book in a lighthouse on Middle Brewster Island. But he couldn't see any code. So he sent the book to a friend who studied old books.

Pinpricks

Snow's friend found 45 pinpricks in the pages. The pinpricks were over these letters.

ABRETUOMAHTAHCDNALSIGN ORTSSEERTTSAEEUDSIDLOG

At first, Snow couldn't figure out the code. He thought he would never find the treasure. Can you figure out what the code says?

Breaking the Code

Then, Snow wrote the letters backwards. He could now read the code. It said:

GOLD IS DUE EAST TREES STRONG ISLAND CHATHAM OUTER BAR.

Snow looked on a map. He found Strong Island and the town of Chatham. He went there with a metal detector to search. After many months, he found a box filled with gold coins.

Some were old Spanish coins. Others were Portuguese (por-chuh-GEEZ). No one ever learned who had buried the treasure.

Sometimes, a code can help you find treasure like the one Snow found. But not all codes lead to treasure. Think of the story of the money pit.

Let's pretend you break a code and find treasure. Is it yours to keep? The answer is not always easy to decide.

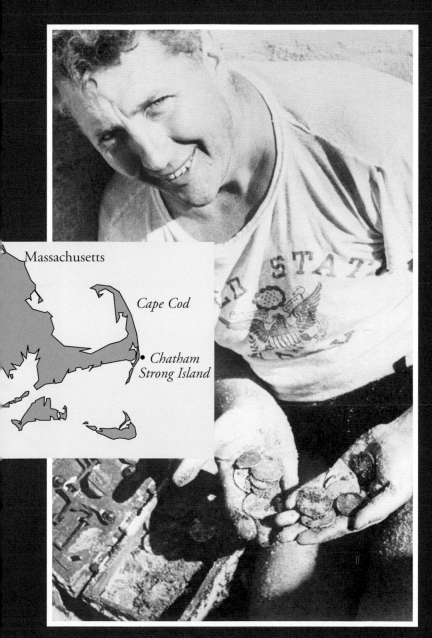

Massachusetts

Cape Cod

• Chatham
Strong Island

*Edward Rowe Snow holds some of
the coins and other treasure he found.*

Items recovered from the
Mildenhall treasure

CHAPTER 4

Finders Keepers

Who gets to keep a treasure once it is found?
Is it the one who finds the treasure? Is it a
government? Does it belong to the owner of the
land? Should a museum get it? What do you think?

Treasure in the Dirt

It was a cold winter day in England in 1942. Snow had just begun to fall. Gordon Butcher was plowing a field for his friend, Rolfe Ford.

Then, Butcher's plow hit something. It was a circle of metal. The circle was big, more than a foot across. He tried to dig it out. Butcher saw marks on the dirty metal. What was this thing? He went to get his friend, Ford.

Whose Gold Is It?

Ford knew **antiques**, so he had an idea
what the circle might be. It could be
treasure from Rome, maybe pure gold. Ford
didn't tell this to Butcher.

The two men dug up the circle of metal.
They also found more old metal things—
plates, bowls, cups, and spoons. Ford took
these items home. He didn't try to sell
them. Instead, he cleaned and kept them.
It took him a long time. But when he was
done, the treasure looked like gold.

Four years later, a museum worker visited
Ford. The man saw the treasure. He said it
was from about 360 A.D. That made it more
than 1,500 years old! He told Ford he had
to give the treasure to the British Museum.

---

antique: a very old object that is valuable because it is rare
or beautiful

A bowl from the Mildenhall treasure

The treasure was worth more than $10 million. Usually, the museum paid the finder for a treasure. But, this treasure had been found four years earlier. And who was the real finder? Ford or Butcher?

The men went to court in 1946. It was very hard to say who should get paid. Finally, the court gave both Ford and Butcher about $1,500.

Tips for Treasure Hunting

Here are some hints for treasure hunters in the United States.

- Know the law for the area where you are searching.

- Ask the landowner if you can search on his or her land before you look for treasure.

- Get the owner to sign a paper that says you will get part of any treasure you find.

- Be careful if you find something. Some treasure is breakable.

- Tell the police if you find any treasure. It might be stolen. If it is, you will have to give it back. You might get a reward.

Know the Laws

In the United States, each state and city has its own laws about treasure. Even a sunken treasure might belong to a nearby landowner. Or, it might belong to the state. If you look for treasure, it's a good idea to know the laws.

Know what to do when you find treasure. If you do the right thing, you may get to keep the treasure or get a reward.

Is there any treasure still worth hunting for? Yes! Read on for just a few examples.

People are still searching for gold in the streams of the western United States.

— Chapter **5** —

Still Missing

Could you find some treasure of your own? Lots of treasure is still missing. Keep your eyes and ears open. You might find a secret code. You might see something glitter underwater or in a cave. You might hear a story about treasure. Here are some true stories of missing treasures. Will you be the one to find them?

Death Valley Gold

In 1862, treasure hunter Charles Breyfogle and two friends were on a treasure hunt. They had camped in the Panamint Mountains in California. The area was dangerous. There were stories of robberies and attacks.

Attacked!

One night, the men were attacked! Breyfogle's friends were killed. He escaped. But soon he got lost in the dark. Breyfogle wandered into the Death Valley desert.

Breyfogle walked for days in the desert heat. He was thirsty. Finally, he found a stream. As he drank, he saw something glitter. Breyfogle thought it was gold. He dug out as many rocks as he could carry.

Breyfogle still was lost. He felt sick and had a fever. At last, he came to a ranch. He was just outside of Austin, Nevada. Breyfogle had walked more than 200 miles (322 kilometers)!

Rock streaked with gold

When Breyfogle got well, he took the rocks to an expert. They had gold in them!

Breyfogle tried find his way back to the stream. He found the camp and his dead friends. But he never found the stream.

Many people have looked for this gold. Did the stream dry up? Did a landslide bury the gold? No one knows.

Death Valley

The Great Lakes

Not all sunken treasure is lost at sea. Some is lost in lakes. The Great Lakes in the United States and Canada can be very stormy. Many ships have sunk in these lakes. Not all have been found.

Minnesota

Lake Superior

CANADA

Wisconsin

Lake Huron

Lake Ontario

Lake Michigan

Michigan

New York

Pennsylvania

Illinois

Indiana

Lake Erie

Ohio

THE GREAT LAKES

Missing Ships

Here is a list of some of the ships and treasures lost in the Great Lakes.

Missing Ships of the Great Lakes			
Ship	**Sank**	**Lake**	**Treasure**
The *Lexington*	1846	Erie	gold worth $70 to $300 thousand
The *Superior*	1856	Superior	gold and silver worth $40 thousand
The *Pewabic*	1865	Huron	gold worth $1 million, copper worth $700 thousand
The *Chicora*	1895	Michigan	gold worth $50 thousand

It won't be easy or cheap to find these treasures. But even today, people are looking. The **lure** of lost treasure is very strong indeed!

---

lure: appeal; attraction

Epilogue

The *Atocha* and the *Santa Margarita*
The Marquesas, off Key West, Florida, USA
FOUND—Worth $200 to $400 million

Roman Treasure
Hoxne, England
FOUND—Worth $2.8 million

Celtic Treasure
Snettisham, England
FOUND—Worth not known

King Tut's Tomb
The Valley of the Kings, Egypt
FOUND—Worth not known

The *Whydah*
The Atlantic Ocean, near Cape Cod, USA
FOUND—Worth $400 million

"The Money Pit"
Oak Island, off Nova Scotia, Canada
STILL MISSING—Worth not known

Gold Coins
Strong Island, off Cape Cod, USA
FOUND—Worth not known

Roman Treasure
Mildenhall, England
FOUND—Worth $10 million

Gold
Death Valley, USA
STILL MISSING—Worth not known

Glossary

antique: a very old object that is valuable because it is rare or beautiful

cargo: a load of goods carried by a ship

dock: to bring a boat up to a platform built over the water

equipment: special tools needed for some purpose

hieroglyph: a character used in a system of writing made up of pictures and symbols

historian: a person who is an expert about events of the past

key: a low island

log: the record of a ship's voyage

loot: something stolen or taken by force

lure: appeal, attraction

mend: to fix or repair

metal detector: a tool used to show that metal is present

mysterious: hard to explain or understand

reef: a ridge of rock, coral, or sand that lies on the bottom of the water

skill: an ability that comes from training

tackle box: a container where tools or equipment are stored

tidal river: a river whose water level changes with the tide

tragedy: a very sad event

Bibliography

Claybourne, Anna and Caroline Young, eds.
The Usborne Book of Treasure Hunting. London,
England: Usborne Publishing, 1999.

Dahl, Roald. *The Mildenhall Treasure.*
New York: Alfred A. Knopf, 2000.

Platt, Richard. *Shipwreck.* Eyewitness Books.
New York: Dorling Kindersley, 2000.